YOUNG PROFILES

Leonardo DiCaprio

Lori Kinstad Pupeza
ABDO Publishing Company

visit us at
www.abdopub.com

Published by ABDO Publishing Company 4940 Viking Drive, Edina, Minnesota 55435.
Copyright © 1999 by Abdo Consulting Group, Inc. International copyrights reserved in
all countries. No part of this book may be reproduced in any form without written
permission from the publisher.

Printed in the United States.

Photo credits: AP/Wide World; Shooting Star

Edited by Paul Joseph
Contributing editor A.T. McKenna

Library of Congress Cataloging-in-Publication Data

Pupeza, Lori Kinstad
     Leonardo DiCaprio / Lori Kinstad Pupeza.
     p. cm. -- (Young profiles)
     Includes index.
     Summary: Highlights the personal life and professional career of the young
native Californian actor, Leonardo DiCaprio.
     ISBN 1-57765-322-X (hardcover)
     ISBN 1-57765-334-3 (paperback)
     1. DiCaprio, Leonardo--Juvenile literature. 2. Motion Picture actors and
actresses-- United States--Biography--Juvenile literature. [1. DiCaprio,
Leonardo. 2. Actors and actresses.] I. Title. II. Series.
     PN2287.D4635P86 1999
     791.43'028'092--dc21
     [B]
                                                 98-39494
                                                   CIP
                                                   AC

Contents

Leo 4

Profile of a Young Star 6

Growing Up 8

Before Stardom 10

First Roles 12

First Big Break 14

A Challenging Role 16

More Movies 18

Leo Mania 20

Staying Grounded 22

Titanic 24

Leo as Himself 26

Fun Facts 28

Glossary 30

Internet Sites 31

Index 32

Leo

Actor Leonardo DiCaprio is one of Hollywood's hottest stars. The 24 year old has worked in four television shows, nine films, and has been **nominated** for both an Academy Award and a Golden Globe Award.

It's hard to look at a newsstand without seeing him on the cover of at least one magazine. He's worked with some of the best actors in show business, like Robert De Niro, Diane Keaton, Meryl Streep, Gene Hackman, and John Malkovich.

Recently he played a leading role in the hit movie *Titanic*, and it seems to be just the start of a long acting career for this young talent. "He is the most gifted young actor I have ever seen," said superstar Sharon Stone, Leo's co-star in the movie *The Quick and the Dead.*

Leo in Titanic.

Not only does Leo have great acting talent, but he also is a caring person. In July 1998, the heartthrob visited gymnast Sang Lan. She broke her neck during a warm-up vault, and was **paralyzed**. While in the hospital, Sang Lan said she would love to meet Leo, and he made her dream come true. He's generous with his time and money. He gives to charities and remains close to his family and friends.

Leo as Jack Dawson in Titanic.

Leo with Meryl Streep in Marvin's Room.

Profile of a Young Star

Leonardo Wilhelm DiCaprio

Birthday: November 11, 1974

Birthplace: Los Angeles, California

Mother: Irmelin DiCaprio

Father: George DiCaprio

Siblings: Stepbrother, Adam

Residence: Hollywood, California

Height: Six feet (two meters)

Weight: 140-150 pounds (64-68 kilograms)

Education: John Marshall High School through his junior year, then worked with a tutor once he began acting more often.

First TV role: the sitcom *Parenthood*

First Movie: *Critters 3*

First Big Break: *This Boy's Life*—he was chosen out of 400 actors.

Leonardo DiCaprio

Growing Up

Leonardo DiCaprio's parents George and Irmelin lived in a poor neighborhood in Hollywood, California. Leo was born on November 11, 1974. Less than a year later his parents separated, but remained close. Despite their separation, they wanted to be in Leo's life. In an **interview** he said, "My parents are so a part of my life that they're like my legs."

Even though Leo grew up in a dangerous area, his parents tried to shelter him from it as best as they could. George and Irmelin would drive him far distances to good schools and bring him to cultural events and museums.

Even as a child, Leo had an onstage **personality**. He was outgoing and funny, and hard to control. When Leo was three, his mother brought him to a taping of a **popular** TV show called *Romper Room*. It wasn't long before he was thrown off the set for acting too wild. Leo remembers going crazy at the sight of himself on camera.

"They just couldn't control me," he said. "I would run up and hit the cameras." This was just the beginning of the young actor's career.

Leo early in his acting career.

Before Stardom

Leo's excitement for acting continued as he got older. School wasn't always easy for young Leonardo DiCaprio. He admits to being teased and called Leonardo Retardo. "I wasn't **popular** at school," he said. "What I would do in order to be more popular was put myself on the line and joke around and be wacky and funny, and I was always known as the wacky little kid."

Leo was more **comfortable** acting out in front of his class than sitting behind a desk doing homework. His parents noticed this and got him a few acting roles in TV commercials. He worked in commercials for Matchbox cars, Disney, the U.S. government, and a few others.

Leo loved being in front of a camera. He says that his parents never pushed him into acting. On a television **interview** he said, "I knew I wanted to be an actor for quite a long time . . ." It wouldn't be long until Leo's dream came true. In 1988, he got an acting role in his first television show.

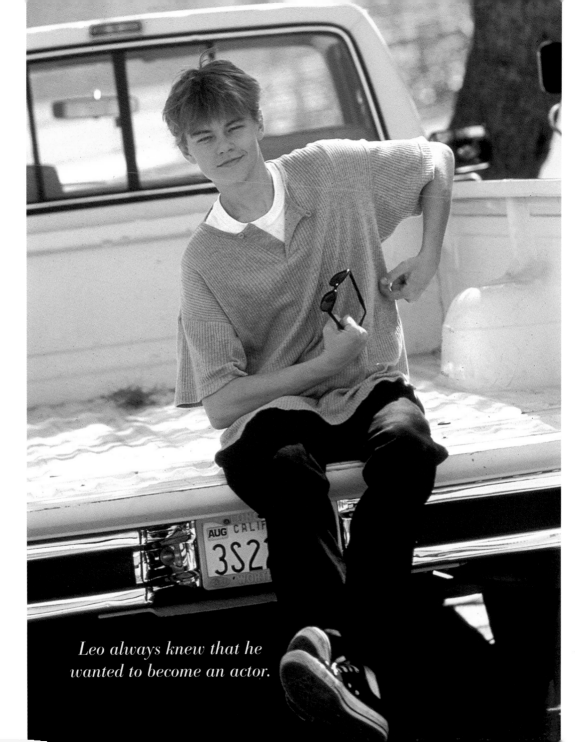

Leo always knew that he wanted to become an actor.

First Roles

Being a class clown seemed to lead him into an acting career. The first TV show he worked on was *Lassie*. It wasn't long before he moved on to the **soap opera** *Santa Barbara*, where he played the role of a teenage **alcoholic**. It was hard for him to **memorize** new lines everyday. After he was done working there, he admitted that he never wanted to work on a soap opera again.

He later was a guest star on a TV show called *The Outsiders*, and appeared on the hit comedy *Roseanne*. Then in 1990, he was cast for a sitcom called *Parenthood*. Even though the show was dropped after four months, fans couldn't forget Leo's face. Leonardo found himself on the cover of teen magazines for the first time.

In 1991, he not only landed a role in his first movie, but also a role on the hit sitcom *Growing Pains.* The movie *Critters 3* turned out to be a flop, but working with the cast of *Growing Pains* turned out to be a good career move. Viewers loved Leo. He received around 300 fan letters each week!

Leonardo in the hit TV show Growing Pains.

Opposite page: Kirk Cameron (L) with Leo.

First Big Break

Leonardo's acting career was just beginning, and the fans were already **noticing** his wide smile and **confident** blue eyes. Now that he had more acting **experience**, he decided he wanted to try working in more movies.

In 1993, his big break came when he was chosen for a starring role in a movie called *This Boy's Life*. He was picked out of 400 young actors. At only 17 years old, he would be working with two **extraordinary** actors: Ellen Barkin and Robert De Niro. Most actors could only dream of working with such elite performers.

Leonardo DiCaprio with stars Ellen Barkin and Robert De Niro.

Leo remained calm about working with the big stars. "Of course, I was nervous at first," he admitted later on. "But if I stayed terrified for too long, it would take away from the film." DiCaprio received lots of praise for his acting. The New York *Daily News* said, "This is the breakthrough **performance** of the decade . . ." Leo says he's most proud of his acting in *This Boy's Life*. With such a star performance, it wasn't long before he moved on to another movie.

Leonardo (R) and De Niro in a scene from This Boy's Life.

A Challenging Role

Leonardo DiCaprio's next **performance** on the screen showed how talented an actor he really was. In 1993, he played a **mentally challenged** boy in a movie called *What's Eating Gilbert Grape.* To prepare for the **audition**, Leo spent a lot of time talking to and video taping children with mental **disabilities**.

Leonardo playing a mentally challenged boy in the movie What's Eating Gilbert Grape.

He said that the character Arnie had the combined **mannerisms** of many different children whom he met.

Even though the whole cast did a wonderful job in the movie, Leonardo's acting stole the show. Movie critics were saying that DiCaprio was

one of the finest actors of his generation. He even earned an
Academy Award nomination for Best Supporting Actor.
Although he didn't win the Oscar, he became one of very few
actors to be **nominated** at such a young age. He loved the
challenge that the role gave him, and every critic loved his
performance.

*Leonardo DiCaprio (L)
earned an Oscar
nomination for his role as
Arnie in the movie* What's
Eating Gilbert Grape.

More Movies

With two hit films under his belt, Leonardo DiCaprio was on top of the world. Between 1993 and 1997, he played in six other films.

In 1994, he starred in a 20-minute film titled *The Foot Shooting Party*, which was so small that it wasn't available for everybody to see. In 1995, he played a leading role in the western movie *The Quick and the Dead*. Even though the movie didn't do well overall, Leo outshined all of his costars.

Leonardo in Basketball Diaries.

Also in 1995, he starred in *The Basketball Diaries*. The movie was about a real-life writer and his troubled teen years. The young star's acting once again dazzled movie critics.

A third movie in 1995, *Total Eclipse*, was Leo's most daring role so far. He played the role of a French poet from the 1800s who abused alcohol and drugs. Yet again, the critics loved his **performance**. In 1996, he was busy with two movies. He played in both *William Shakespeare's Romeo and Juliet*, and *Marvin's Room*. After two more great performances, people couldn't stop talking about Leo.

Leonardo in Marvin's Room *with costar Diane Keaton.*

Leo Mania

Movie critics weren't the only people who loved Leonardo DiCaprio. Fans started **noticing** him too, and it didn't take long for a Leo-craze to start.

Everywhere Leo goes fans scream his name. Friends and family members have seen him chased out of restaurants and clubs by Leo-crazed fans. A person who once worked with Leonardo said, "Wherever he walks there is a gang of people, 10 deep, who want a piece of him."

How does the young star feel about all of the attention? "There's pressure, that's true," he said. "It's becoming difficult for me to have a private life." While at a hotel in New York, a photographer saw him through a window and begged him to smile for the camera. "No," Leo said through the glass. "I don't want you guys making me do anything. I want my privacy."

Being mobbed everywhere that he goes has made it hard for him to stroll unnoticed through a public place. He has a bodyguard to fend off screaming fans. Leo may have to dodge frenzied fans, but he never forgets his friends and family.

Leonardo DiCaprio and his family.

Staying Grounded

Leonardo is getting big rewards for the films he's done. Some say that he's asking for almost $20 million for each film he works in. He flies across the globe and mingles with some of the most famous people in the world. There have been four books on the best-sellers list that were written about him. How does he handle all the fame? He seems to find comfort in his family and friends.

Although some people who turn into big stars forget about those closest to them, Leo has held on tighter than ever to his mom, dad, and grandparents. He also hangs out with the same friends he had before he became famous. Leo tries to spend as much time as he can with his family and friends despite his busy schedule.

It wasn't long ago that he moved out of is mother's small three-bedroom home, which is close to where he grew up. His mother admits, "I can't see him as other people do. All I'm concerned about is his health—he should sleep more, exercise more, eat better. . . . The rest, I wouldn't care if he gave it up tomorrow."

Leo and his mother remain close despite his busy schedule.

Titanic

The film *Titanic* was an instant hit. It was the number one film for 16 weeks, which is longer than any other film. Leonardo DiCaprio was **nominated** for a Golden Globe Award for best actor. The movie brought in over $1 billion to movie theaters around the world.

Leo and Kate Winslet in a scene from Titanic.

Leo played Jack Dawson, one of the leading roles in the film. His costar Kate Winslet played Rose. Kate said of Leo, "He's probably the world's most beautiful-looking man."

Leonardo was excited to be in *Titanic*.

"I'd never done a movie like it," he said. "You arrive on the set and you see thousands of people who are involved with it—it's just such a gigantic thing. You've got to keep a sense of yourself and of your character at all times and not **concentrate** on the wild madness that's going on around you. It was a completely different **experience**."

After *Titanic,* Leo played in another movie called *The Man in the Iron Mask.* It came out just after *Titanic* and Leonardo was hotter than ever. Because of Leo's role in the movie, *The Man in the Iron Mask* was number two at the movie theaters. Leo played a leading role in both the number one and two movie at the same time!

Leo in The Man in the Iron Mask.

Leo as Himself

Despite the mega-hit movies he's played in, Leo remains true to himself. He only acts in the movies that he thinks he will do well in. He doesn't let other people decide for him what is right.

When questioned about drugs, Leo said, "I'm absolutely clean. I've never tried anything." He enjoys the nightlife and going out with friends, but says, "I don't want to be thought of as a party animal . . . I'm not like that." Leo grew up in a rough neighborhood and saw drug deals going on near his home. He knew he didn't want to be a part of it.

Leo has worked hard to become an **exceptional** actor. He has played in many well-known movies and wants to keep acting. Leo once said in an **interview**: "I'm just getting going. I told you before—I'm just starting to fly."

Leonardo DiCaprio

Fun Facts

Nicknames: Cappy, The Noodle, Leo

Pet: Bearded dragon lizard named Blizz

Favorite Sports: Baseball and basketball

Favorite Sports Team: Los Angeles Lakers

Favorite Book: *The Old Man and the Sea*, by Ernest Hemingway

Wish in Life: For everyone in the world to take care of the environment and live in peace

Quotes:

"I'm not really the quiet type . . . but I am the rebel type in the sense that I don't think I'm like everyone else."

"I don't have emotions about a lot of things. I do get excited, but I don't get overly sad or happy."

"I won't stay cooped up in my hotel room [hiding from fans]. I don't want to give up the life I have."

"Friends and family are really who I am. Everything else is hype or fabrication."

"I'm not the sort of person who tries to be cool or trendy."

Jack (Leonardo DiCaprio) and Rose (Kate Winslet) in the movie Titanic.

Glossary

Alcoholic: a person addicted to alcohol.

Audition: to try out for a play or movie.

Comfortable: feeling at ease.

Concentrate: to think hard.

Confident: to be sure of something or yourself.

Disabilities: something that disables, or stops you from doing something.

Exceptional: above everything else, not like anything else.

Experience: having done something before, having practice.

Extraordinary: something that is not regular.

Interview: to ask someone questions.

Mannerisms: the way a person speaks or acts.

Memorize: to remember something.

Mentally challenged: someone who has an incomplete development of intelligence.

Nominated: voted for.

Noticing: paying attention to.

Paralyzed: to lose movement or feeling in part of the body.

Performance: the show you put on.

Personality: the kind of traits, habits, behaviors, or attitudes a person has.

Popular: to be liked by many.

Soap opera: a type of television show that has an ongoing plot.

Internet Sites

www.leonardodicaprio.com
Check out the official web page of Leonardo DiCaprio. This web page has his biography, the awards he has won, the films he has been in, and more. On special days you can chat directly to the star himself.

www.kcweb.com/superm/l_dicaprio.htm
Learn more about the hottest star in Hollywood. His biography and the latest news on Leo is on this cool site. Chat with other fans of Leo and find out when his next movie will be out.

www.usentertainment.com/celebs/malesdicaprio_leonardo/
Get the latest news on Hollywood's leading man. There are sound clips from different movies that Leo has been in, links to other great Leo web pages, and more!

These sites are subject to change.

Pass It On

Tell readers around the country information you've learned about your favorite superstars. Share your little-known facts and interesting stories.
We want to hear from you!
To get posted on the ABDO Publishing Company website E-mail us at "Adventure@abdopub.com"
Download a free screen saver at www.abdopub.com

Index

A

Academy Award 4
audition 16

B

Barkin, Ellen 14
Basketball Diaries 19

C

charities 5
critics 17, 19, 20
Critters 3 6, 13

D

De Niro, Robert 4, 14
Disney 10

F

family 5, 20, 21, 22,
  23, 29

G

Golden Globe Award
  4, 24
Growing Pains 13

H

high school 6
Hollywood 4, 6, 8

I

interview 8, 10, 26

K

Keaton, Diane 4

L

Lassie 12
Los Angeles 6, 28

M

magazine 4, 13
Man in the Iron Mask, The
  25
Marvin's Room 19

N

New York 15, 20
New York *Daily News* 15
nominated 4, 17, 24

O

Oscar nomination 17
Outsiders, The 12

P

Parenthood 6, 12
parents 8, 10, 22
profile 6

Q

Quick and the Dead, The
  4, 18

R

Romper Room 8
Roseanne 12

S

school 8, 10
soap opera 12
sports 28
Stone, Sharon 4
Streep, Meryl 4
supporting actor 17

T

television 4, 10
This Boy's Life 6, 14, 15
Titanic 4, 24, 25
Total Eclipse 19
TV commercials 10

W

*What's Eating Gilbert
  Grape* 16
*William Shakespeare's
  Romeo and Juliet* 19
Winslet, Kate 24, 29